Notes from Quarantine

One Year of Online Recovery

By Susan G.

First paperback edition April 2021
ISBN 978-0-9970942-5-1 (paperback)
ISBN 978-0-9970942-6-8 (ebook)
Published by Possibility Lady Press
Portland, Oregon
www.thepossibilitylady.com

For Jennifer P., Julie T.,
and the wonderful women I sponsor

Introduction

Before the world went on lockdown in March of 2020, I had been attending four to five meetings of Alcoholics Anonymous each week, and I had been doing that almost every week of my 13 years of sobriety. It was a good schedule, one that kept me balanced and in the middle of structured meetings having a singleness of purpose: carrying the message of recovery from alcoholism. I was a grateful alcoholic with lots of AA friends and sponsees and service commitments.

The last meeting I attended in real life was Monday, March 16, 2020. One week later, I attended the same meeting on Zoom, an online video conferencing platform that was new to me, as it was to most of the people I know in recovery. Within three weeks, AA was on Zoom worldwide, and articles appeared frequently in recovery literature encouraging members to get onboard. Meetings are imperative for most of us to stay sober.

Going to a meeting on Zoom meant many things. Aside from the obvious fact that you aren't really "there," you still see and hear all the participants—at least those choosing to have their cameras on. The learning curve was gentle, and we soon learned the online protocols.

Remarkable things happened. My meeting attendance increased to seven or eight a week. I got to see my sponsor, who had moved 400 miles away. I went to meetings with my son, who has been gone for a number of years and lives far away. I met women in my sponsor family from all over the country and have become close to many of them. I have attended meetings in other countries and have heard the lovely accents of Australia, Scotland, Mexico, and England. I started a newcomer women's meeting that first week of quarantine and there were four of us present. Last week there were some 35 women, many of whom have never been to an in-person meeting; they call themselves "zoom babies." That first baby celebrated one year of sobriety last week. Although my physical world had become very small, my spiritual program expanded dramatically.

This little volume is the record of the notes I took from March 2020 to March 2021. Because I was in my home office, I had pen and paper at hand and soon found myself jotting down things people shared in meetings. I would never have done this in an actual

AA meeting, as I was taught to listen only and not be engaged in other activities, so this newfound freedom to write down what I heard was invigorating and changed the character of my listening. It was more direct, unencumbered by looking around the room at other people and wondering about what they were thinking or wearing or doing or who they were.

Although I did not attribute names to these nuggets of wisdom as they came out of the mouths of sober members, I still remember who said some of them, but most have drifted into anonymity. Some may be familiar to you because we often hear the same sentiments, but these are the words that spoke to me at those specific moments in time. They are arranged into the three familiar categories of What It Was Like, What Happened, and What It's Like Now. Maybe some will speak to you.

Susan G.
07/07/07

What It Was Like

Here is my secret—you can never know how much
I need to drink.

I am addicted to what you think of me.

Alcoholism is a disease of self-neglect that harms me
physically, mentally, and spiritually.

Every drunk is a drink away from a drunk.

I had a baby with a man I didn't like.

The promise of alcohol...

I had to be devastated. I had to be torn apart by the fact that I am an alcoholic.

The lying life

Spiritual bouncer—who do I let into my life and who gets rejected at the door.

I drank a half fifth of Blackout.

I am what's wrong.

In the context of looking good or staying right, did I lower my standards?

Alcohol was my best friend.

I'm a wild guy having a wild time.

I'm an egomaniac with an inferiority complex.

Would I let anyone do to me what I do to myself?

I was dying from the inside out.

Drinking is the manifestation of an inner sickness—
a spiritual malady.

We're good people who have lost our way.

I have no idea why I can't stop drinking.

I forget instantly what it does TO me because
I love what it does FOR me.

My fraudulent face

Alcohol demands attention.

I am my own worst critic.

I thought perfection was love.

I had razor-sharp focus getting to the bar.

I felt I had to keep the party going and was drunk at my own wedding.

I was a bowl of defects.

One drink is too many and a thousand's not enough.

I'm an alcoholic and I want more. I always want
more, even when there is no more.

I don't drink to get high; I drink to get normal.

I was playing in a mud puddle when the ocean was
just over the hill.

Alcohol isn't my problem—sobriety is my problem.

I was in a spiritual wasteland.

I was in spiritual prison.

I was in spiritual purgatory.

I was in a spiritual dungeon.

I was in spiritual torment.

I was in a spiritual abyss.

I was in spiritual hell.

What Happened

The time came when there wasn't anything left of me, and all I had was enough strength to call AA.

I am an alcoholic. You have to just say it. That's the way it is. It's that way because it's that way.

Trust God, clean house, help others.

Work the steps one at a time and in order.

When, not IF, these (selfishness, dishonesty, resentment, and fear) crop up, we ask God at once to remove them.

If this is your lot, are you going to drink?

Come all the way in and sit all the way down.

I learned not to cheat at Candyland.

It's not hard to do it alone. It's impossible.

God walked with me through every room and down every hallway and through the dark doors at the end of every hallway.

I must remain tethered to God.

I get what I need here.

Recovery is progressive.

In AA, you can rent or you can own.

What is important is to begin.

Do you want to be right, or do you want to be free?

Are you willing to take direction?
Are you willing to change?

In Step 10—I continue.
In Step 11—I improve.
In Step 12—I practice.

I take refuge in Step 11.

I can't be found in myself.
I discover myself in others.

Being busy in AA is essential for my sobriety.

God is just a label.
Did you argue with the label on the bottle?

AA takes us from the REEs—resentment, remorse,
regret—to the BEEs—be happy, be joyous, be free.

After the 5th Step, look daily for God to show up.

What does this look like without fear?

AA transformed the baggage of shame and regret
that I came in with into gifts.

I had the gift of the man in the mirror.

We are good people who needed to get well.

My path to freedom is simple—if I'm not the problem, then there's no solution.

Stay well. Stay happy. Stay fierce.

I acted like a kind and loving wife until I became a kind and loving wife.

I have smart feet.

Stick and stay!

There are no insignificant people. There is no one who isn't supposed to be here.

What It's Like Now

Love and compassion

Hold my seat and I'll hold one for you.

I will walk to the edge with you.

The perfectionist in me loves that I can say
"whatever" and "good enough."

We are forces for good.

I am responsible, moment to moment,
for my words and actions.

We are the Ninja sisters, agents of the light.

Faith without footsteps is fantasy.

Being present is a form of meditation.
Listen like your life depends on it.

I will try to make the world better and happier
by my presence in it.

A peaceful mind has no room for feelings of guilt or
shame.

The bliss of blamelessness

27

Give up, grow up, show up.

Every time I say Yes, every time I show up,
every time I share, I don't know whose life I might
be affecting.

The answer is always God. My job is to act out of
my heart with love. God's job is to take care of me.

My spot here is an absolute miracle, and I don't
intend on losing it.

Say Yes!

I can live with problems and not abandon myself.

Wherever you see God, sit in that window.

God's arms are waiting. All I have to do is crawl into them.

I see the capacity for love and hope and change in my sponsees.

The channel is open and my porch is waiting.

Sunflowers turn toward each other.

There will always be those who do better than I and those who will not, and that is irrelevant to who I am.

Emotions are like children—you can't let them drive
and you can't stick them in the trunk.

Next week and next month are other times.
No need to mix them up with today.

I am living authentically as a woman of integrity.

We are no more or no less than what God intended.

Just be.

I'd be honored.

Service is where I need to be.

Acceptance is tied to the moment.

I serve each person God sends into my life.

I can speak from the hole or the whole.

I sponsor sponsors.

Keep doing what you've been doing.

Practice the presence of God.

Even if I get it wrong, I'll get it right if I let go and
let God.

God can move mountains,
but I need to bring a shovel.

I pray in the morning and then need to spend the
rest of the day acting like a person
who said their prayers.

Service is an expression of Love.

I am the only example of Alcoholics Anonymous
that someone might ever see.

If you can't laugh at yourself, you're missing the
biggest joke of the generation.

I have been saved to save.

I lead with love wherever I go.

Love requires an action in order to express itself.
That action goes by the name of service.

I go to meetings because newcomers never
walk by my couch.

I give daily of my time, talent, treasure, and touch.

I keep one hand in yours and the other in God's.

Made in the USA
Monee, IL
22 July 2021